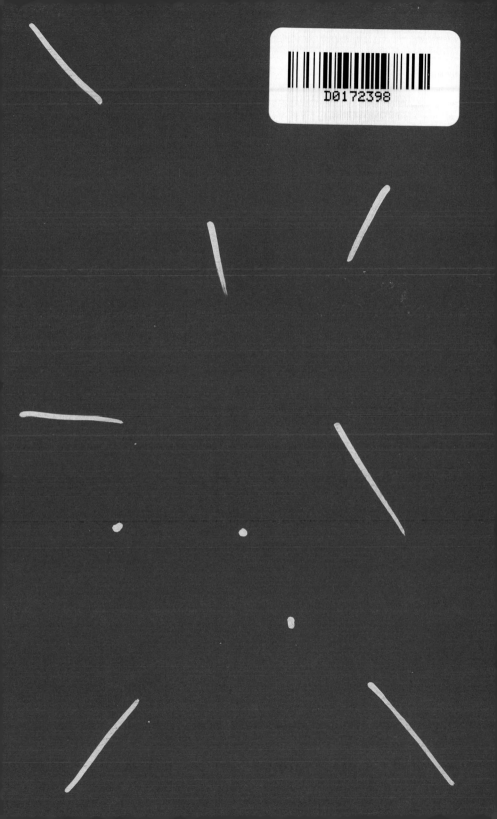

TURNING LEFT
TO THE LADIES

TURNING LEFT
TO THE LADIES

Kate Braid

PALIMPSEST PRESS

Palimpsest Press
96 Stewart St, Kingsville, Ontario, Canada N9Y 1X4
www.palimpsestpress.ca

Book and cover design by Dawn Kresan. Typeset in Adobe
Garamond Pro, and printed offset on Rolland Zephyr Laid at
Coach House Printing.

Library and Archives Canada Cataloguing in Publication

Braid, Kate, 1947–
Turning left to the ladies / Kate Braid.

ISBN 978-0-9784917-0-3

1. Braid, Kate, 1947—Poetry.
2. Women construction workers—Poetry.

        I. Title.

        PS8553.R2585T87 2009
        C811'.54   C2009-901056-9

We acknowledge the support of the Canada Council for
the Arts for our publishing program.

Canada Council   Conseil des Arts
for the Arts   du Canada

In memory of
Jacqueline Frewin, carpenter
and Carlyal Gittens, bricklayer, tilesetter

and for my granddaughter
Zlata Sophia Steeves
in hopes this book will be only a curiosity
by the time she is old enough to make her choices

For Jacqueline and Carlyal

Tradeswomen, sisters,
we were beautiful in our mouths.
Held songs there.

Through the grass beside us
ran shadows.
We walked fearless, singing.

When you stepped away
the rest of us kept walking,
didn't notice

until it was late and dark
and there were two fewer songs left
to guide us.

Table of Contents

Apprentice

Around my hips the stiff leather tool belt
holds me together, ending
in an optimistic buckle clipped close.
The man's gruff command sets me scrabbling
for nails, a level and square,
tools of the trade to which he is native
and I, the woman, am immigrant.

He squeezes the trigger of the saw, a wild screetch
and a smooth glide forward as wood falls,
the exact length. He cuts and bends and lifts and nails
while I fetch. And carry. And watch.

At lunch time I pour tea (my gift, all I can offer)
from my new blue thermos. He drinks,
acknowledges with a nod and returns to work,
slow dance. He doesn't see my delight.

Now you, he says. I lift the saw, sabre-toothed
demon, mirror his stance, model the lift
of his shoulders, the set of his hands.
High scream of power, hot tang of pitch,
the grit of sawdust—and again.
The tool belt hugs my hips, hammer solid at my side

until the saw slips, makes one bass roar and jerks, dead.
He doesn't have to look, knows by sound.
A frimer grip, he orders. *Don't push!*
Again I bend and set my saw's teeth to waiting wood.

Hammer

Of all my tools it's the hammer
    that comforts, inspires, leads.
When I lift it from the loop of my belt,
    its soft soughee of wood leaving leather
is a prayer, another strong hand.

And whether I merely tap at drywall
    or sweat over spikes and two-by-tens,
I love its rigid strength, cool power ascendant,
    ease with which it moves walls,
drives nails with equal grace.

Cold poured steel, hickory grain,
    titanium ti-bone, curved, long, straight,
rip claw, curved claw, drywall, sledge,
    setting hammer, raising hammer, finish, framing—
the lift and fall of it—gentle persuader.

I see my hammer rise
    through blue flecked space, irresistible.
I have learned to let it do its work,
    not push or nag or waggle my wrist but
let my shoulder guide my hammer to its mark.

Lesson 1: Nails

Look at Ed over there.
Sixty if he's a day and the man looks
more graceful than a goddamned
crane. Nails hum for him.
Walls rise all around him
like some Eastern palace.
Ed knows
these little lines of steel can talk,
tell you what kind of wood you're dealing with,
how thick and whether it's wet or dry.

You feed 'em to your hammer like this.
Are you right handed? Hammer in the right,
nails in the left. Don't look!
Just finger those nails and
roll them like cigarettes.
Place them
one at a time fast, right
where your hammer is
waiting, poised at the top
            of the next swing
to give them a love tap or two.

Got the rhythm, kid, you got it now?
You've got to love a job that's got
this much rhythm,
this much swing.

Spy

I parachute into man's country,
hoist beer in the bar as if native.

Cool, I talk shop, stand as they stand,
not quite sure
of the cocky swing of hips,
lift of the glass in a loud bass,
confident, laughing.

This is the world of the knowing.
It's only a small slip under the radar
when I turn left to go to the Ladies.

Song and Dance

Framers flash hammers, a dazzle of dervishes
slick with the oil of our sweat, we improvise a quickstep.

If only the foreman could see us now! We're a pirouette of steel toes
a chorus line of carpenters tap dancing nails into place

daredevils coaxing conga lines of concrete.
We're centre stage with a harmony of hammers, a polka of plywood

cha cha of chamfer a waltz of waler and wedge.
Come quick! It's a whoopee! We'll finish this house

while the boss isn't looking, a labour of love.
It's a hip hop *glissando accelerando* a cakewalk of wood-laden love

and who knows where we'll go in this framing fandango
this foxtrot of fascia this *plié*, this *jeté, olé!*

Nail

She's a joiner, a social little thing always wanting
to get the parts together, two-by-tens to plywood
two-by-fours to each other, a romantic
she aims for a clear connection
but any join will do.
Her motto is
No moving!
When she's
here whole
buildings
appear.
She is
common
and cheap
but we
love her,
comes
from a
large
family
with
musical
names
like
ardox.
Don't
get in
her way
for
with-
out
her
whole
cities
will
fall.

Lesson 2: The Partner

You give 'im hell, girl! Get tough.
Sure, you got a peanuthead for a partner but
trust me—when he says those things,
pull yourself up tall, tell him to fuck right off.
Say it nice.

Guy like that, if he's such a genius,
ask him why he's not in college?
You know why it's important, don't ya' kid?
We're not talkin' ha-ha here, we're talkin'
safety, talkin' your life.

A partner's gotta be there for you.
A good partner is the guy you rely on,
the mustard on your sandwich.
You tell this guy he shapes up or else.
Tell 'im Ben sent you.

Concrete's Coming

Concrete
is a wrestle with your lover.
It's got that kind of weight
that kind of almighty.
It might be love,
it might be a fight.
You know the feeling
when he comes
up the lane with a sigh,
a groan and a shift in gears.
Are you ready?
Concrete's coming!
And here we go
with not another thought
except
to get it all in place,
those surprising moments
when he's come up
with the unexpected—
a little flood here
a false step there
tears and sweat and
time for
grappling hard physical
in it up to your eyeballs
water
everywhere
the slippery of wet
and calls for more!
more!
Speed now
of the essence and
quick! It's setting up!
Then finding ways to slow it

down, give you time
to enjoy the smoothing out
seeing how
it's going
good for all of you
the surprise once more
of taking that wild beast
shaped nothing of might
and pouring it into moulds
that tame it,
thrill you, make you
forget yourself all over
until it's in, it's
done
and you're moving
slow now.
Time for laughter,
grin and say
good one,
relief deep to your
muddy boots, wonderful
and cleansing
as it sits there glowing grey
and solid and all in place
and I think I love you.

How the Angels Learned About Concrete

Behold the Heavenly Host
descending from on high
to land on concrete

                thud,
and the earth shakes
with a shimmer of divine expectation.

Angels are looking to see how we mortals mix
our lighter-than-air concrete,
perfect, perhaps, for Pearly Gates.

The foreman solemnly reads the genesis of Concrete:
how Rock begets Pumice and Gravel, Gravel
begets Sand, Sand begets Shale and Cement.

Angels send the good news back—
down here we mix concrete incarnate,
do it all day for the masses.

After work the angels skip bread and wine
for coffee and doughnuts at the Red Rose Café.
Nothing like sugar to bring you down to earth, they chime.

They play the hit, *Heavenly Host*, on the jukebox,
carol along in chorus, wonder
if the Maestro can hear from this far away.

They're a little out of tune, tired
from a long day's work
while the jukebox thunders

Come on Down and
It's My Party and I'll Cry If I Want To
'til a guy in a leather jacket asks where they're from

and his buddy whispers back, *They're Heaven's Angels.*
I've heard the guys in white are even tougher
than the ones in black. Better not cross 'em

and sends another round of doughnuts,
instructions to the boss
they're not to be messed with.

When the waitress asks, the angels assure her it all tastes
divine. She pours coffee without end,
says, *Tell me when.*

The angels smile sweetly.
'Til Eternity, they say, feet planted firmly
on concrete everlasting, amen.

A Geologist Addresses the Carpenters' Convention

You boast Concrete is not for the weak,
that she's urgent when she calls, irresistible—
but have you considered her mother, Volcano?

Volcano is the wild woman of the rock family.
Promiscuous, she can't be bound, flaunts herself
in front of Concrete who waits demurely in trucks,
waiting to be told where to harden up next.

Volcano is shameless, Fire goddess who'll embrace
anything, anybody, erupt
over the flanks of mountains
unlike her grey daughter, Cement, a good girl
who mixes politely

with water, stays within the lines, measures
as ordered and hardens quickly
so everyone can go home without wondering
where all this wildness will end.

If she catches you, Volcano will take you
to her molten breast. Staring out through clear black glass
you will not recognize yourself
dreaming of the next time, wishing for mere Concrete
as you cool.

Say the Names

Say abrasive.
Say abatjour, abutment and adze eye.
Say aggregate and air-dried cement, say
alabaster anchor blocks, anhydrous lime and
antemion. Say apprentice, with an arabesque.
Say arris at the place two edges meet and
eyes up to the architrave of the door
and the artisan who built it.
Say ashlar and auger, avoirdupois and azimuth.
Now bridge to badigeon and ball peen,
to beams and barefaced tenons.
Embrace barefoot joints and bargeboards,
bezel and batter board.
Chant bay, bead and reel and bead and butt moulding,
bell-hanger's bit.
Belay us a benchmark, bevel to bias.
Don't stop now—say bleeding tile, blind mortise,
block and tackle. Bring on board and batten, bolts
and bond stones.
Then there's buck and built-up beams and
burl, butt hinge and still
we're only on the b's because this building,
this building is concrete bloody poetry.

How She Knows

On Monday
when the men ask what her husband thinks
of her being a carpenter
and she says she's not married,
then they ask what her father thinks

then she knows.

On Tuesday
when the men don't tell her the new safety rule,
won't tell her how the drill bit disconnects
so she can do the job they've ordered her to do,
when they speak in whispers watching her then suddenly laugh,
when they invite her for a beer after work
and take her to the strip joint

then she knows.

On Wednesday
when she says she needs a 69 inch length of board
and the men flick their tongues in and out,
talk porn

then she knows.

On Thursday
when the men write Fuck the Ms. on the bathroom wall,
when someone drops a wrecking bar from eight feet up
on the place she'd been working seconds before and
when the men can't make her quit

then she knows

they will lay her off on Friday.

Trophy Woman

When I ask him why his locker must be decorated
with this photograph of naked female flesh,
he says it's because he must have this
thing
      of beauty.

Why not flowers? I ask. But no.
Women can't understand it, he says.

She won't leave me, this woman, her body
pinned to his wall like a hooked fish
and him the hunter whose body longs to pierce,
the power of his long finger
beckoning with fish hook and spear.

Mine is the experience of prey,
of the fish and the deer, of being entered into,
of a space within meant for welcome.

Once, even the hungriest hunter honoured, gave thanks.
But this hunter hates. I know it by his sudden silence
when I come near, his hooded glance.

I walk away just a little afraid
of the man who follows a few feet behind.

Day's End

The body, our great ally,
knows what it's here for.
　　　　　—Carole Glazer Languille

I shed clothes
put on something that feels
more like skin

wade through a warm body of air
to slip between pale blue sheets
of water

suspended
on a tenderness of bubbles
yield

to the slither of wet over
shoulders, belly, thighs. Liquid
forgetfulness.

A prayer of water
briefly burning
shines through me.

One arm lifts, slow roll,
deep breath and the grace
of a long smooth stroke goes on

and on
to a sleek exhaustion
of limbs, liquid centre.

Post-Modern Breasts in the Bath:
After reading Robert Priest's "Post-Modern Penis"

Everybody has nipples; not everybody has tits.
—Zonko (Bill Little)

these rose balloons
proud galleons
leaders
bobbing on
before
bloom
with energy
enthusiasm
estrogen
co-conspirators
bouncing buddies
twins
of the flesh
flaunt
the circle
shy
buds blooming
bright radishes
awake
to a rising beat
with the warmth of heat
and hand
cows in their cud
a child might draw milk
like water
from the well
of these breasts
welcome
to the hills

and cave
of my dark spaces
cell small
all meat, all matter
my also
my body
my self.

The House Renovates the Woman

takes her dreams

    and builds upon them

demands

    decisions

building

character

    the house

        moulds her body

           by acts repeated

zen times

she cannot build

    without bending

humbled

  has

    visions

    of how things might be

      working from the bottom up

obeys the goddess of gravity

mathematics of structure and strength

book of changes

grows taller, her feet

on the earth

clearly

her strength depends upon it.

Pinker

I was suspicious of pink. Pink said:
you're a girl, don't run, don't rock the boat,
be a little lady.

I was the dirtiest guy on the job,
splashed through puddles and whistled my way
to a fat pay cheque every Friday.
The sticker on my hard hat labelled me
Wild Woman.
My muscles grew strong as whole buildings rose.
I told my friends, "I built that."

But one guy liked to drop things on my head,
and one guy just wanted to protect me
for my own good.
One guy couldn't wait to tell me
his best dirty joke and one wished
I'd drop dead
(but it was nothing personal)
so I started to wear pink.
First, little pink embroidery flowers so small
you could hardly see them on my coveralls,
then a pink mackinaw, a pink plaid shirt and tomorrow
I'm gonna paint my lunch bucket—
you guessed it.

The Hairdresser

I was determined not to talk.
Sitting in pink pearl seats I was too old
to be seduced by the legends of this place
where "girls" giggled and told all.
Not for me those false confessions;
I had my women's group.

But slowly, the words escape
like air from a tire under pressure, past
reluctant lips so that finally I sit, grateful
as Victoria winds pink and purple rollers in my hair,
cheers my dream of a late return to school
and whispers that if I go without the blowdry
I'll save a little on the budget.

Slowly we slip into celebration, small rituals
only strangers may observe.
She covers me with robes, unguents, the incense
of a hot perfumed rinse. I join chants
of *Not too short! Not too curly!*

I seek her now, small but steady solace I escape to
in the middle of a knot-tied week, this meditation
of cut and clip and curl until the ceremony
closes with an amen at the cash register
and I drive home smelling of the merest touch of gel,
wondering why I denied for so long
the sympathy of another woman's hands in my hair.

Mother of the Lacrosse Goalie

Tonight is the big game. Kevin is nervous, misses the "soft" ones. (Mothers learn this language slowly. Kevin has explained the terminology, patiently, more than once.)

Last week a ball hit his head and he toppled neatly, all six-foot-five of him, straight as any soldier in a slow motion descent. The crack of his helmet on the cement floor was a rifle shot in the suddenly quiet arena and when both teams began to brawl, my son was an innocent hostage. I didn't rush to battle to save him because his father held me to my seat. All part of the game, he insisted.

As the game pounds on, Kevin is "uneven." (This is his father's term. I think it means playing well for five minutes, fading for ten.) In the end, his team loses.

At breakfast the next morning we sit at the kitchen table, in my territory now. You seemed nervous last night, I say. He shrugs. This is what goalies do.

When you feel anxious, I tell him, you need a strategy. What I have learned is to pretend I am a tree. (Ignore his raised eyebrows. This is important. It took years to learn this.) I pretend my roots go deep in the earth, holding me steady. Then I can handle anything.

There is a moment's pause. He grins. *I know what you mean, Mom*, he says. You do? So quick, this clever child. *Yeah, about strategy. I come out of the net and hit somebody.*

Hit? I repeat it stupidly. *Yeah, on the back of the legs, or yell at the ref. It's connection, Mom. You make connection. Isn't that what you mean?*

Is it? This child of street fights who embraces the world with his body. Over and over he has explained that when you are big, as he is, people pick on you as a test. Of themselves. It's what boys do, he explains again—when I can't understand it, when it is different for girls, for me.

And suddenly I see the men I work with—carpenters, electricians, plumbers—all in their own way, making the connection physical. Who cares if, by my measure, it is not always gentle?

His face now is alight and waiting. Yes, I nod and swallow. That's it. In our own way, we all have a strategy. In our own way, all make connection.

Connections

All day I build houses, hammer home
spikes, ring nails, join
joists to plywood and stud, pour
concrete, lay it right, finish
satisfied.

All night I dream
that the minute I turn my back,
hang up my tool belt, the boards behind me
open their mouths in a slow wooden O
as nails slip out, rafters fall,
recover, return to tree.

All night each stone, each grain of sand
in my foundations shivers loose
and slips away.
Bolts, nails, screws, all clamour to leave, line up
to return to the cool shade of brown boxes,
or better, to mother rock.

Every morning I approach my building, surprised
it still stands, nothing changed
apparently.

But all day, beneath the thin sheath of progress
my body registers the slow hum of wood and metal,
knowing this is temporary
and they wait, just wait,
to go home.

Touching Tools

Why don't you wait? the computer technician asks. *This will only take a minute.* I'd rather read a book, I say, rather not feel incompetent in someone else's trade. Fix it and call me when it's over.

Too late. Already he has picked up a screw driver, undoes four screws that hold the case. He moves at a slow and steady pace, holds his tool at the exact angle to catch each screw as it falls. He performs these acts to a body he knows well.

And the body responds, the shell sliding easily away as he touches the insides here, and here. I recognize craft. I see skill. Within minutes he finds the flaw, shows me how the wheel in the hard drive doesn't swing as it ought.

And now by the grace of his screwdriver, by his touch on the tools, by the way he makes it look so easy as the tiny wheel spins back to life, by all this, I can't say no. As water flows for plumbers and current for electricians, as buildings stand for carpenters, so this man makes things electronic, hum.

When he lays down his tools, I watch the moment of separation with regret, long to have him touch them again, with his hands, give grace.

The Window Man

His doctor says it's too many years
of the high-pitched screech of saws on aluminum
and sure enough,
the window man tells us at coffee break
that last time he went to the symphony
a whole crew of violinists made elegant sweeping gestures
with their bows, bodies bent as if to meet gales of music,
but no sound came to him.
The man who makes windows,
who lets light into other people's lives,
has his own ears stopped, must sit and watch music
as if behind glass.

New Houses

the new houses composed themselves
—Jane Hirschfield

In the arms of carpenters
new houses shiver and creak, embrace wood

compose themselves: here a roof, a window
there the coldness of a door, opening.

Earth grows used to space retold.
But at night, alone, sometimes we remember

each house is a small violence to the earth.
And why not? we stubbornly ask. It's that

or the human heart unprotected.
Still, it's why every carpenter carries

in the pocket beneath her hammer, secretly
a small black stone, to remind her.

The Feeling of an Angle

[I] have known the abruptness of corners too,
the pivot, the silence.
                    —Stephen Dunn

i.

I have known the abruptness of corners, snap
of chalklines that tell me when to turn, how far.
I have known the peppermint of straight-ahead lines
where floor and wall and roof all march
upright under my hands in a no-nonsense parade.

Can't argue with the facts—two nineties drive a straight line
of Protestant progress to a still-to-be-built horizon.
When the direction is forward,
no questions are asked.

My eye measures in straight lines now. Anything less
is suspect. Round, unthinkable.

ii.

The feeling of an angle:
cornered.

iii.

Four corners of a room, edges of a two-by-four, the rise
of steps—all tyrants.

Ninety degrees fits awkward but after awhile
feels almost normal in the bowl of my hips.

I cut another straight line, pause
to glance at the clouds now and then
when just for a moment, I yearn for curves.

Both Sides: 1

It isn't rational
how much I love this job
building the big things.
Little reasons that may mean nothing
to you, like being out in the weather
until weather becomes
a character in my life
having its rough days
and its great ones, like the rest of us.
Simple things like feeling my body strong
and graceful doing the things
other carpenters do, performing
the magic of hammer and nail
building something, together
that will last for the rest
of our lives.
Little things.

Both Sides: 2

It isn't rational
how much I hate this job,
the terrible loneliness, sobs
stuck in my throat, the men
who watch my every move
as if to catch me
imperfect. They punish me daily.
How I hate those times of hiding
I'm a woman, the times a thought pops up
uncensored, when I'm tired
or feeling good, an unmanly thought,
like the time I suggested potluck
for lunch. That time they liked it.
Other times they hate me
for reminding them of difference.
Those times I am wax melting
in the heat of their hatred.
Some gentle man once told me
every hand has two sides.
I show only one.

Autobiography of a Nail

Driven, I enter every crevice, push
into your darkest places, leave no trail.

When it rains I turn rusty and slow
but when sun shines I blind you
with connection.

I am forged in fire.
Only those who know me well, know
I am too easily bent.

Remembering Medusa

When I was a girl I was properly taught
to fear the enemies of men,
like that monster, Medusa,
who turned sailors to stone.

But when my partner at work threw his hammer
and narrowly missed my face (accident, he said)
then dropped a sledge that barely missed me,

when I asked how he was and he answered,
Life is a bitch and then you marry one.
After he blamed me for everything
that wasn't perfect that day, saying,
Nothing personal, it's just you're a woman,

then I began to see things
from a more Medusa point of view.

I'm thinking I might invite her round,
spend an afternoon in the garden
drinking peppermint tea and talking.
Sailors have nothing on construction workers, I'll say
and she'll agree, accept a ginger snap, feed it
to her right, writhing ringlet.
Perhaps you could teach me a thing or two?

and next time a carpenter opens his mouth to insult me
I'll use her trick, another man petrified
to perfect silence
as the bricklayers carry him off
mistaking him for stone
while I smile a perfectly Medusa smile.

Construction Quilt

With their slogans
        bitch   cunt   whore

the men
        punch   pierce   rip

        the soft fabric of my self.

They spit words like nails,

        their cheeks ripple with curses.

When I duck behind deafness

        they hit harder.

At night

        the needles of their jabs
                draw blood.

I use it

to pull the broken pieces
        together,

    with my woman's hands,

        mend myself

with a thin red thread.

Cuntada

There's too much glory to the phallus. Why can men write about their sex, penises erect or not, the size thereof and

whole chapters on the noble male member as lingam and sword, the family jewels, while we women have nothing to show except breasts of course but those aren't the heart of the matter I mean the core, essence, absolute fact of life real thing innerspace-deepness of our other heart, innermost residing home country, our inboard where you come right down to it. Cunt is spoken with a spit and mere mention of vagina leaves most people incoherent but

incoherency is inarticulate I say, so if we can't mention it without getting turned inside out all puckered up like trash and not a nice word to say, really working at it but oh bone dry then getting back to the subject you can't see, maybe we should throw rivers of words over our female sexual organ, hub, kernel, our visceral *chez nous*, the one at the center of it all— let's talk about women's sex.

Let's talk about our private parts, our genitalia and loins, our uterus, clitoris and womb, vaginas fuscia pink and royal red. Let's talk about moules and *yonis* in a foreign tongue, take a lifetime to cheer our bikini bizkits, our cherry pops, to cha cha our honey pots our hush-puppy-sacred-scoop-passion-fruit quims. Here's a toast to our pink taco rose garden our Southern belle tongue magnet wunder-down-under French pleat our velvet triangle and hail the vessel of life the gateless gate our sweetgrass bed our bent berry alter, our nest.

Wonder at each box of assorted creams, our baby bear sugared almond, our pearly tongue. All glory to this vessel large as a cathedral, delicate as a mouse's ear, our sacred space, centre, cunt.

Norman Mailer Needs A Dictionary

A macho man, Norman says,
must be impregnable.
I look it up:
Not capable of being entered by force,
unyielding.

Impregnable: an adjective,
a word used to limit, a word
dependent or subordinate.

Impregnable lies somewhere between
impractical and impress
but struts ahead of its cousin
impregnate.

Impregnate: a verb,
an action word for women meaning
make fruitful, fulfill.

Norman should look it up.
Impregnable,
right there in the dictionary
after impotence
and impoverishment.

Taking Work Home

We can hide in our trade. It's why we love it.
—Comment by a tradesman

It's easier to handle a two-by-four than an emotion.
Two-by-fours don't talk back, don't contradict. One cut
makes what I want, the way I want it. One nail
and it stays put.

At home, emotions slide. Even buried alive, they rise.
No matter how hard I work, each day must end
and my heavy boots return
to a sullen welcome, another fight.

At work the rules are clear: if wood resists, hit harder.
Small act of force committed daily.

So last night, at home, trying to make my feelings fit
in the only way I can measure—I hit
then I hit harder.

I Used to Drink

not gaily,
but with
a whiskey hammer every night
that drowned
the dullness of a day spent
denying
the things that were woman of me.
Small thing, the men said.

The taste was bitter

but easier
than pulling out individual pinpricks
of pain.

> *I wouldn't let my wife do this.*
> *Want to see a dirty movie after work?*
> *Fuck 'er.*

Once I drank
all night, so
in the morning, gold
everything looked—didn't it?—
brighter?

Red wine, brandy, scotch or gin
it didn't matter. All poultices.

Desperate not to drink alone, I'd
beg, jibe, challenge, jeer,
anything
to make you keep me
a wet, a weary company.

Don't leave me, I said,
terror like an awkward duckling
rising roughly off its pond.
What right have they?
I swallowed harder.
A double.

So many terrors:
the terror I might not be able to do this,
the terror that maybe they were right
(only a woman and all that).

I drank as if I were a flower, dried up
and seeking rain.
I drank as if it would open a closed vein
of wonder.
I drank as prayer, as petition,
as penance, as plea.

I like you now, the other carpenters said.
I like you soft, a little unfocussed,
a little loaded, not all that
unladylike push and buzz.

Drunk, I acknowledged anger.
Went home.
Dead sober.

Tin Woman

I am a tin woman
tempted by nothing.

When the wind blows
it sighs, thin whistle through me.

I am absence, a hollow woman, shell
fit tight. Don't come close. It marks me.

Terrified by the wilderness in rain
I ache for the oil of blood.

My laugh is mechanically
correct. I cough rust and cold air.

If you lay your ear to my armoured chest you will hear
a carefully crafted construction of emptiness.

Why I Stay In the Trade

Because I love to feel my body taut and lean.
Because I love to see things grow.
Because the men know so much more than me.
Because I want to know it too.
Because I find the men—how they do—desperately inviting.

Because they will not let me.
Because it's only fair I should be allowed to try.
Because I'm stubborn.
Because I'm angry.
Because no matter how hard I try I'll never reach the end.

For the approval of my father, the pride of my mother.
For my sisters. My brothers.

Because muscles.
Because it's fun. Because I love big and hard.
Because concrete. Because dirt.
Because I want to be all of me.
Because.

The Beauty of Men

It is not violence but muscle—the force to do—
curled and bent and burning
inside.

They deny it. Hide it. Rip it out
with hammers and knives and guns, even crosses
if they have to.

These are the signs of the beauty of men:
set jaw, the shimmer of muscle
eager to lift beyond any limit, lost

in the wild pleasure of motion. They will move the world
with their own two hands, force it if they have to, doing
what mere thought didn't know had to be done.

Drilling

At work, they're drilling a hole
in my veins. Lorne lays out my arm
carefully, measures
two points on my wrists and circles them
concentrating. He picks up the drill
with the extended auger bit.
We'll need the extra length, he says
and positions the point
over the first pencil mark.

The sharp metal tip tickles
and only then do I worry.
Be careful, I remind him,
knowing he's always careful in his work—
it's one of the things I love about him.
Lorne grunts, concentrates on getting
the bit perfectly vertical from all four sides.

At work, they're drilling a hole
in my veins, stringing me up by wires
so the crane can lift me to the thirteenth floor,
just another part of the structure.
Every building is baptized in blood.
It's only the girl, after all.

Hurry, the foreman says. *We gotta finish
by lunchtime. It's not a piano!*
My body is on the line. And now
for production, for progress,
I rise.

Bikini Angel

The first time I saw her was like a dream, a vision of thick black glasses, upswept corners set with fake diamonds reflecting light like sun from her eyes. Old and wrinkled with skinny legs, skinny arms, she wore a yellow bikini, blue hard hat. It hurt my eyes to see her, etched above yellow lumber carved against a deep blue sky.

Bikini! I exclaimed, thinking burns and slivers, male eyes. *Freedom of motion!* she seemed to say and disappeared in a puff that could have been welder's smoke.

But the next time a man on the site thought trouble, she shook a warning finger he felt as a twinge of pain. *There's that arthritis,* he said and forgot about me.

One little old lady in a yellow bikini, grey hair tucked high in a bun, poked the labourer's conscience to clean up around my saw, gave the back of my boots a tap when I stepped too near an edge. On days my partner balked and didn't want a woman in his brotherhood, when I slogged through mud and cold, I'd catch a glimpse of yellow around some corner over the top of a pile of golden lumber and I was not alone, I swear it. Sometimes I heard a breeze as if a voice in my ear whispering, Yes, you belong.

At first she came often. When there was danger, hooked my fingers a little higher for a firmer grip, led nails into wood like water. When someone cracked a thoughtless joke she winked and made me laugh.

I see her rarely now but I know she's there, a little old lady with knobbley knees dancing along the high lace beams of the crane like sunshine.

Talking Trades

One day working with Joel I feel too good,
forget to be careful.
When the next board fits perfectly,
I call in a voice loud as his,
That's how I like it—nice and tight!

Tradition cracks.
I dare you, my eyes say. Now you know I know
your secrets. I am making them mine.

I watch, in case he chooses anger.
Joel leans forward, holds my gaze, gives me
one long slow wink. *You said it sister!*
and we nail the board home
nice and tight, the way we carpenters like it.

The Talker

We're an odd pair, we carpenters.
One white woman, one native man—
Chatterbox and Silence.

We're nailing the roof when I spot the new foreman.
A clanging army of one, he yammered and yapped
all through breakfast how he'll be doing things differently.

There goes the new guy, I say.
Spark in a powder keg, I say.
He talks too much, I say.

George's eyes fix on the next nail, the rhythm
of his arm steady as it lifts.
Guess he just wants to be heard, he says,
and brings the hammer down hard
on the nail's head.

Most Radical

When I have been on a construction job
for six months and
the men count me as colleague,

when the sun is shining
and the breeze blows
and the walls are going up
and we're joking back and forth,

when we've finally accepted
each other as comrades,
carpenters

then it is a miracle,
the impossible made flesh
and this is simply the most radical thing
I have ever done.

Man-Womanly

It is not enough to be manly alone or womanly alone.
—Virginia Woolf

It's another basement job, good for sledge hammers,
some distant tenant's idea of beauty split now in a dozen pieces
while I swing my hammer through clouds of dust,
protective yellow muffs over my ears.

The owner's three-year-old watches for a while
from the safety of sidelines, then a small voice
distantly heard between blows, *I have earmuffs too,* he whispers
and runs upstairs to return with his winter wear, earmuffs
with the face of a stuffed bear, brown button eyes perched
each side of his head echoing his own dark velvet eyes.

Then, *My finger nail hurts. Would you fix it?*
He brings scissors, lays a small pink hand within my large one, rough
with the day's dirt.

I kneel beside him, two heads bowed over one small finger
as I cut the offending nail, brown bear earmuffs caressing my cheek,
sweet child's breath an incense above us both, mended.

If a Hammer Were to Yearn

Art happens when a tool tries to become an animal.
—Don McKay

It would be a bear, heavy one of the deep voice
and large importance, leaving its prints.
Hammer scat.

Saw is a mountain lion, sharp teeth hovering over wood,
a bit beautiful but mostly mean.
Ready to pounce.

Nail is the mosquito that yearns for fresh flesh
of lumber, enters stinging with a fine needle.
Sharp love.

These children of rock and tree prowl, steely with a wild hot breath,
yearn to wander outside the edges, be born again.
Feral.

Rough Ground

Memories of all those summers spent sweaty
in the blue jeans, T-shirt and hammer crowd,

stripped to the bare essentials of an arm, a back, an eye.
The same but different and aching

from the loss. Nothing feminine about this path.
I carve each step as I walk it.

I am barren.
The men blast me with their not-knowing.

Something sweet is gone. The juice and heft of me
is twisted, dried by the effort, desperate to drop.

Feed me, feed me
with something green and growing.

Vive Le Poulet Libre!

The truck ahead of me on the highway
is filled with chickens;
live ones, white
thousands of them fluffed
against the winds of doom as they fly, caged
along the 401 headed
we-all-know-where.

It's the end of the line for those chickens.
We all know that too,
so why has one silly bird stuck her head
out of the unstrapped corner of her cage
dog-like, as if to sniff the breeze.

Back turned on her cowering sisters,
her head is up and into the wind,
a Hell's Angel wild chicken, flaunting it
from the deck of a 500 cc Mack truck.

At the stoplight she opens her beak,
lets loose a long wild cackle.
O joie de vivre among chickens!
She is, what the hell, just along for the ride,
a good-time, not a long-time chicken.

Oh foolish bird to defy your fate!
Oh heroine to declare your chickenhood!
Eagle of your class, I salute you
and honk a long wild blast on my own small horn.

The Female Form

See that kid in the white T-shirt, the one
with a pack of Players rolled in his sleeve,
he called me "carpenteress."

He must have noticed
bare metal where the leather of my steel toes
scraped plywood, giving me the open-toed look
for summer.

Perhaps he picked up on the classic lines of this pink
plaid shirt, fifty cents at my couturier, the Sally Ann.

Or he noticed the touch of colour at my neck
where the inhalator drapes softly from the black rubber straps
leaving a carpenter's blush.

No? Then surely it was the turn of my curls set off
by the pert yellow hard hat, the cheerful upturned brim
also helpful for shedding rain.

But of course, it must be the gloves I wear for unloading lumber,
this season's bulky look, squared off and casual,
the colour of my eyes accented by mud.

Carpenteress—yes. I work hard at it, this look
of the great outdoors, doing the work of men
with a special fashion flair.

December Carol

Last day of the job before Christmas and we're all sent home
with a fat bonus in our pocket and a turkey in the pickup truck
into the early darkness of December under a
rolling over creamy mother-of-pearl moon
so bright she's bouncing off a navy blue sky and *Jupiter*
playing loud on the stereo, warm inside
with splashes of Holtz, the truck easy, airborne
when just as I turn the corner, above the street
the wide arms of the crane working overtime,
laughter with Christmas lights running blue and red and green,
draws a fat finger over the West End of the city,
swinging wide for one last load until
just as *Jupiter* reaches its peak, the finger stops
and points straight on to that full onion moon
and all the galaxies line up, harmony at last,
all is calm, all is bright
tonight, as I swing on over, going home.

Construction Worker

She stands on scaffolding four stories up,
attached to the stone of an ancient tower by steel,
her own structure, built with her own two hands
making space.

Far below, pale faces strain and marvel,
reflections of a bright sky.
She hovers between them, suspended,
one hand on rock, one hand on its sister
sun-warmed steel.

Now holding tight, one breath and she lifts a heel,
taps once, twice, on the plank that holds her.
Bolder now, a toe, a foot and up
she rises scuffing two feet at once, two hands
solid now, sun shining, faces
blinking up at her as she takes
another breath (the vertigo of birds)

raises her arms, her hard hat in salute and sings
into light and air.
From here, she can see everything.

First Weeks Back in Construction After Seven Years Away

Week 1

It never used to hurt like this.
I've forgotten how to move.
I trip, drop lumber, tools.
Measurements add up to zero: zero comprehension, zero skill.

Blueprints are an X-ray of a building's bones and I'm a doctor
seven years away from my practice. I gaze blankly at blue smoke.

It's worse when I forget to act like a man, forget to pretend
I understand everything and pray for quitting time.
When there's a job I don't want I stick around, humiliate myself
by asking, like a woman, instead of going for long walks, like a man.

I actually ask for help.
If they ever doubted it, the other carpenters know now.
I celebrate Friday by cutting through the main water supply.
Can you see my shame?

Week 2

It returns. Slowly
my body remembers how to walk, how to lift a saw,
how to be apprentice to motion.
I swear at the right times.

Some things have changed. After all these years,
I have somehow learned assertiveness. No one bothers me.
I was a younger woman then, trying too hard to fit in.
Now I don't care what the men think.
I do uncarpenter-like things like bake cookies
for the crew, who dub me Employee of the Month.

When no one else is around I tell stories to the apprentice,
how it was for me. He has never heard such talk, such honesty,
such ignorance. Just like his. He didn't know
you could be yourself—even sometimes—on a job.

Week 3

I have remembered what I once did well.
I measure, cut and nail. I say the right things
to clients, help the foreman make the job go easy.
I laugh at bad jokes. Make good money.
I have what I need. And know
there are other things in my life I need to learn now,
other things to remember.
Though it is easy, I will not do this again.

Thirteen songs to my hammer and one lament

1.

I never speak her name aloud for she
is a dragon, tough number with a raspy roar
of smoke-stained steel.

2.

Hammer. When they are mad the men say it slow
so it sounds like hammer-her. They want to let me have it
between the eyes.
I am silent, just trying to get by.

3.

Her name distilled
is all the steely hard names the men have ever called me.

4.

Her name lifts me, says, we're still here,
together.

5.

I am the only carpenter on this job
who calls her hammer, *She.*

6.

This is the day for the pink plaid shirt, strawberry perfume
and swinging my tool belt, hammer on my hip hard
as I waltz to work. *Hi boys! It's me! And my hammer.*
I dare you.

7.

What else is like a hammer,
more right and faithful, more reliable?

8.

Mishandled, she bites back. Over time
gets cranky, tears the tendons of my hand, my forearm,
'til they ache, take longer each night
to forget her.

9.

Her name is red, is rich, is the smell of pitch,

10.

in broad daylight kisses the heads of nails,
a wet smack to the two-by-fours, deep
belly wrench suck sexual thrill
of two-by-tens.

11.

The girl, men say, not noticing there are two of us.

12.

I dream a man curses me, watches me walk
to a plank resting across sawhorses.
I raise my hand and BANG! two pieces fall to the ground.
The man is speechless.
My hammer does this for me.

13.

Gun, the men say to their air hammers, air gun
steely bleak to my shredded ears.
Give me the quiet of my hand hammer,
small stitches, lacing.

14.

Though it's all memory now.
Hammer, here's a sorrow song of goodbye,
a sister song from my hard-hammering heart,
your name my secret still.

Something Lost

These days, construction workers are small
hard-hatted jewels dangling
from the necklace of a crane.

Sometimes I slink past, head down as if
ashamed. I have lost my right to be there.
Sometimes I wave—*Hi boys! Remember me, a sister?*

They never wave back. Or if they do,
it's one of those waves they give to all the girls,
a whistle, a leer.

I have lost something—the smell of pitch, the certainty
of nails. Those men? They were a magnifying glass
in which I saw myself, tenfold.

Falsework

It's the work that supports all the other work,
invisible in the end, when the Mayor cuts tape,
proclaims it done.

Whole crews do nothing but build it
carefully. We assume its strength,
climb on thin limbs of aluminum and steel
as if they were our own.

The people who build it are the minions of the trades
like the secretaries, clerks, receptionists in my other life.
False work we say and pay them less
for what won't show.

Stepping Out

Making a spectacle out of oneself can be a political strategy and an act of courage.
—Curatorial notes,
Elizabeth Carefoot exhibit

Why yes, I am overly large with size ten feet and a sixteen on top why yes, I am frequently known to kick things, knock things off their centre, all out of whack into a new alignment goddess forbid oh I could be sorry now doesn't that look a bit better I sort of like it that way when I climb up ladders I like to grab hold hard hug those siderails and clamp my feet tight to the rungs I'm up there like a spider and over the top ready for anything pick up my load before old Lorne can protest throw it over my shoulder and the man's shouting Don't do that it's heavy! and what does he think I'm getting paid for the same as him and secretly I heard him tell Jim he's feeling the cold these days I notice he doesn't yell very loud when there's anybody else around so I'm into my size ten steel toes ready for action all these big steps I'm taking I want power love those big plaid jackets the men wear I got myself a pink one they sure noticed I sewed little colours and flowers with embroidery thread all over the front and Judy over at the shipyard uses nail polish in a wild way and her sister Claire put butterflies in glitter on the back and the boys are reeling now I notice they clear their throats when I roar for lumber got to keep those labourers moving the walls going up I think I'm building the Tower of Babel only this one's gonna stand it's that woman's touch my own she-brand of feminine and we better get cracking girls 'cause we've got one heck of a lot of catch up building to do the world is just dying for our touch let's see those she-women build let's hear it for us!

Building the New World

When she thinks no one's watching,
Shannon practices looking cool with a hammer,
practices feeling strong.

Oi-Lun dares lift her eyes, looks further
into the forbidden. Nicky builds doorways
for her entrance into the world.

For the first time in weeks there's a light in Kathy's eyes.
I like this, she says and remembers
the dad she barely knew was a carpenter too.

Maggie dreams of a shop of her own, a safe place,
helps Carmel plan the furniture she'll build
while Suzanne listens to the silent surd of light.

All of them add new meaning to the word homemaker
as we build the new world
on nail, one wall, one woman at a time.

Notes...

Page 20: "How the Angels Learned About Concrete"
Traditional concrete is a mixture of cement powder, water and heavy aggregates such as sand and gravel. When the cement and water are mixed with lighter aggregates such as expanded shale, vermiculite or pumice, the concrete weighs less and is called lightweight composite concrete.

Definitions and terms for "How the Angels Learned About Concrete," "Say the Names" and "Falsework" are from R.E. Putnam and G.E. Carlson, Architectural and Building Trades Dictionary. Third edition. (Illinois: American Technical Publishers, 1974).

Page 23: "Say the Names"
The phrase, 'Say the names" is from the poem, "Say the Names," by Al Purdy, published in Beyond Remembering: The collected poems of Al Purdy (Madeira Park, BC: Harbour, 2000).

Page 24: "How She Knows"
The graffiti, "Fuck the Ms" thanks to Marcia Braundy.

Page 26: "Day's End"
The epigraph is from Carole Glazer Languille's poem, "Five Doors."

Page 38: "New Houses"
The epigraph is from Jane Hirschfield's poem, "All Summer You Kept Trying to Answer."

Page 39: "The Feeling of an Angle"
The epigraph is from Stephen Dunn's poem, "Corners."

Page 60: "If a Hammer Were to Yearn"
The epigraph is from a comment Don McKay made at a reading at Douglas College in New Westminster, British Columbia, years ago.

Page 73: "Falsework"
The definition is "Framework, usually temporary, such as bracing and supports used as an aid in construction but removed when the building is completed."

Page 74: "Stepping Out"
Epigraph is from the curatorial notes for the Elizabeth Carefoot
exhibit held at Simon Fraser University, Burnaby, British Columbia
in 1991.

... and Thanks

In 1977 I got my first job in construction as a labourer on a small
island off the coast of Vancouver, British Columbia. I was blessed.
Never in my wildest dreams did I plan to be a construction worker
much less a qualified carpenter but I was desperate to stay on the
island and I'd run out of money, along with all the options a woman
usually has for work. Secretary, waitress, receptionist—nobody
needed anything like that. What they needed was physical labour,
craft skills, and everyone knew women don't—women can't—do
that. One night at a party I told a few friends I was going to have to
leave because I couldn't find work and one of the men said, "I just
quit my job as carpenter on the new school. Apply for that."

The new school was the biggest job going. It hired a steady
rotation of men (all men—this was 1977) who'd work a while and
then, in the casual way of island labour, take a break knowing the
work would probably be there again when they needed it. When
the man said "carpenter," I froze. It was inconceivable. Besides, "I
don't know anything about carpentry," I said, very reasonably given
the party was in full gear and I'd had a little too much to drink and
smoke. "All I ever built was a flower box." Besides, who'd ever heard
of a woman carpenter?

"Lie," the man said. And every guy in hearing distance, nodded.

I could never quite get a poem out of that moment, but in spite of
the "Lesson 1" poem in this book, "Lie" was my real first lesson.

And that is how it began. Thanks to a canny foreman (who later told
me the men had been slowing down and he hoped they might show
off if there was a woman around), I got that job, which eventually
turned into apprenticeship—a four year training period that gave
me a Journey Carpenter ticket with Red Seal Certification. Later
I would join the Carpenters' Union and when there was no union
work, run my own renovation company, Sisters Construction, with

Chryse Gibson and later, Jacqueline Frewin and Gina Horrocks. Later still, I taught carpentry construction at the BC Institute of Technology (BCIT).

But first I would stumble through the thickets of being a woman— the only woman for a long time—in a "man's job," certainly, in a man's world.

Most of these poems were written toward the end of my time in construction and shortly after, when I was still somewhat battered by the experience. Men and women still have a lot to learn about working together in blue collar work. But the joys of physical labour, the joy of building, kept me trying for fifteen years.

In some ways it feels strange to be going back to this time in my life. I give the poems to you now for two reasons. First, because it's a reminder that women can do this work. But more importantly, because there was something important there that still needs to be told. The reader, I hope, will
understand what that is.

Several of these poems have been previously published, often in slightly different forms and with different titles. I am grateful to the publishers and staff of the following journals and anthologies: *Antigonish Review, Arc, Canadian Woman Studies/les cahiers de la femme, CV2, Dandelion, Edgewise Café* (e-zine), *Event, Fireweed, Labour: Studies in Working-Class History of the Americas, Left Bank, More Than Our Jobs: An Anthology* (Eds. Glenn Downie and Pam Tranfield), *On the Level, Our Times, Poetry Canada Review, Warren and Nancy at Pooka Press, Rocksalt: An Anthology of Contemporary BC Poetry* (Eds. Mona Fertig and Harold Rhenisch), *Thru the Smoky End Boards* (Eds. Kevin Brooks and Sean Brooks), *Taking Action: A Union Guide to Ending Violence Against Women* (Eds.Deborah Prieur and Mary Rowles, BC Federation of Labour and Women's Research Centre), *2000% Cracked Wheat* (Eds. Edna Alford, Robert Currie and Don Kerr) and *Tradeswoman Magazine*. "Concrete Fever" was published as a broadsheet by High Ground Press. "December Carol" won second in the Acorn-Livesay People's Festival (Lapointe Prize) and section ii. of "The Feeling of an Angle" was reprinted as a postcard poem by Pooka Press.

"Song and Dance" is written with thanks to Lorna Crozier for "Radishes."

"How the Angels Learned About Concrete" is for George McWhirter.

"Say the Names" is the title of one of Al Purdy's last poems. This poem is for him, with thanks not just for all the poems, but for showing me you could be Canadian, and alive, and still be a poet.

"The Hair Dresser" is for Victoria.

"Mother of the Lacrosse Goalie" is for Kevin Steeves.

"Touching Tools" is for Dave Dillabough.

"The Window Man" is for Russell Smigelski.

"Man-womanly" is for Patty Osborne and David and Travis Streb.

"Construction Worker" is for Tom Wayman.

"First Weeks Back in Construction After Seven Years Away" is for Colin Boyd.

"Stepping Out" is for Judy and Claire Kujundzic.

"Building the New World" is for the women in the 1995 Women Exploring Trades class at the BC Institute of Technololgy.

In "Cuntada," my gratitude to Carol Shields' *Larry's Party* for phallic research and to the women of The Poetry Compossibles, to Joanne Arnott (in Mother Time) and to Dawn Kresan, publisher of Palimpsest Press, for fearless research on the uterine side.

Thanks to Seamus Heaney whose gritty work in *Seeing Things* inspired several of these poems.

Deepest thanks to all blue collar women, especially those in Vancouver Women in Trades, without whose strong hearts I could never have stayed so long at the work I loved. Thank you too, to all the men who hired me, worked with me and taught me their skills, many of them with grace, especially Ray Hill, Ted Bowerman and Jack Carpay.

Thanks to the members of my very first writing course at the Kootenay School of Writing with Tom Wayman, and to dear Tom who got me going, gave me confidence and pushed me to send out the first poems for publication. Tom is the father of Canadian work writing and those of us who write about our work—and who see the enormous importance of writing about our work—owe him a debt we can never fully repay. Thank you also to the women of my long-time artist's group, SexDeathandMadness, who buoyed me from the writer end, particularly Sandy Shreve who remains a poet-sister and wise critic. Thanks also to George McWhirter and Patrick Lane, to Betsy Warland who has a carpenter's eye for structure and beauty when it comes to poetry and to Dawn Kresan for being tough. Especially I thank John and Kevin who put up with the messier side of things, when it spilled over at home. My love to you all.

About the Author

Kate Braid has published four books of poetry: *Covering Rough Ground*, which won the Pat Lowther Award, *To This Cedar Fountain*, nominated for the BC Poetry Book Prize, *Inward to the Bones: Georgia O'Keeffe's Journey with Emily Carr*, winner of the Vancity Book Prize, and *A Well-Mannered Storm: The Glenn Gould Poems*. With poet Sandy Shreve she edited *In Fine Form: The Canadian Anthology of Form Poetry*. Kate has also written, co-written or edited three books of non-fiction, and her essays, articles and poems have been widely published and anthologized. More information can be found at www.katebraid.com.